VERSING THE MYSTERY

Versing
the Mystery

POEMS BY
CHRISTOPHER VILLIERS

AROUCA
PRESS

ISBN 978-1-998492-02-2 (pbk)
ISBN: 978-1-998492-03-9 (hc)

Arouca Press
PO Box 55003
Bridgeport PO
Waterloo, ON N2J 0A5
Canada
www.aroucapress.com

Send inquiries to info@aroucapress.com

CONTENTS

PART I

Sonnets
from the Spirit

❦ MY EVE

I named all the creatures of the earth,
But who would call my name upon it here?
Who would share my garden? Enjoy my mirth
With me? Whose touch would give me comfort near?
The sun sank down; my lonely soul took rest,
Sleeping with dreams of warm tender desire,
God heard my yearning and took from my breast,
A rib to make a woman, me inspire.
Bone of my bone, flesh of my flesh, my star
Shining on me, my own beloved Eve,
Together we shall live, however far
Life takes us, your side I shall never leave.
Spring of my soul, I drink your love so sweet,
All that awaits us we shall as one meet.

❧ NOAH

Under a slab of sea the earth shall slip,
Into death and birth, all things are ready,
I hope the animals behave on ship,
We draw up the door and our nerves hold steady.
Rain crashes hard against the land, tiling
With water over stone and soil, building
A worthy grave below the sky, piling
Judgement upon the world, green waves gilding.
Evil must drown so that the good may breathe,
I did God's will, no trying to debate
An execution, my old world must leave.
Trusting to come to a better state.
We float as all around us sinks from view,
Trusting in God's promise to start anew.

ABRAHAM AND ISAAC

I go out now, to kill my chosen son,
He who has given him so takes away
His promise, orders that completely stun
My soul, yet God's commands I must obey.
"God will give us a lamb," I speak kind lies
Or desperate hope, faith beyond reason.
We plod on under grim expectant skies,
To where I shall commit father's treason.
I bind him ignoring his pleading face,
Doing God's will in loving horror here,
I raise my knife against my future race,
Then the Lord's angel interrupts my fear.
Untying him, sighing with him, I give
God his ram, and in tougher faith I live.

♪ MOSES

Bush burning into me strange words of flame,
The One who is consuming me entire,
Upon this mountain tells His sacred name,
And takes my life to live within His fire.
Back to Egypt I must go, my people free
For their ancient God, claiming their new land,
Shedding their old skin, long-worn slavery,
For brave new life held in God's own hand.
Through my crooked doubts He shall build straight roads,
His wonders work through me, His powers shine,
I shall have Aaron bearing speaker's loads,
To persuade the people to drink this wine.
I tremble down the mountain to begin,
Another life, and Israel's battle win.

❧ BALAAMS'S ASS

Wretched man! Always beating me so hard
For such little things—but still I saved you.
Against the sword-angel I stood your guard,
For which you beat my backside back and blue.
For once at last I got to answer back,
Then you saw the angel who set you straight,
Lowering the staff you had raised to smack,
Struck by the shock into a wiser state.
You had to bless what some would have you curse:
Israel over its jealous neighbours,
To wish them better though kings wished them worse,
God's holy will drives the prophet's labours.
And so this donkey assisted God's grace,
Remembered with love by God's chosen race.

❦ RAHAB

Strange men came into my house all the time,
But I never expected Israelite spies,
In Jericho I was treated like slime,
I leapt with joy at this pleasant surprise.
With prostitute's cunning I hid them well,
Under the flax hid salvation for me,
Their Lord was mighty, His triumphs did tell
A death warrant: here was my discharge fee.
Life for life, I saved them, gave them a rope
To climb out of the city, to prepare
My old world's destruction, a new world's scope.
My kindred sworn safe, I did not despair.
A crimson cord our protection secured
From the slaughter: now we sing to the Lord

❧ SAMSON

One last time, Lord; please give me one last time,
My gouged eyes seek some vengeance, please let
Me repay the Philistines for their crime,
And through crushed pillars my pains forget.
I betrayed my blessing to the sly girl
With teasing eyes, I have paid my price
Give me back some change, let me once more hurl
My strength against your enemies, those lice.
A false god praised by a false people proud,
Mocking us both, You must defend Your Name,
My hair returns, join with it strength unbowed,
Letting me now die with them to end my shame.
Yes, strength singing, the stones begin to crack,
Death shall deliver what my life did lack.

HANNAH'S PROMISE

My womb a hollow desert, yawning wide
Swallowing my dreams of motherhood whole
Long yearning nights I lay down and cried
Urging my body to fulfil its role.
His other wife taunting me, mocking my
Emptiness, he just stood deaf to my pain
Stabbing me with each child's face, at each sigh
Torn from my throbbing flesh, driving insane.
I go to the Temple to make my plea
Murmur desperation into God's ear
The priest thinks I am drunk, rebuking me
I set him straight, he says my dream is near.
A son, fruit of hard faith, my wound healed
Sworn to God's Temple, a promise sealed.

𝄞 DAVID'S CALLING

Half-forgotten in the fields, I watch sheep
Be sheep, my brothers doing God knows what,
I see no lions but try not to sleep,
Or shrivel up, this afternoon's so hot.
A strange summons, some priest wants to inspect
All my father's sons, even this small runt,
I wash my face and look with some respect,
At whatever shall prove that odd man's hunt.
Old priest, eyes still sharp, rising towards me,
Then pouring an oil, a king's anointing
On the youngest son, this I cannot flee,
Though brothers splutter at this appointing.
I did not seek but God now calls me in,
To reign for Him; another life begin.

♪ SAUL

Israel has one Lord—and me as its king,
An awkward enterprise, what am I for?
I did my best, I thought, fit tributes bring
In sacrifice, but no that's not God's law.
Slaughtering Philistines just like cattle,
Regaining Israel's promised lands in might,
Defeating Amalek in fine battle,
Am I so worthless? Was old Samuel right?
I am no easy servant, that is sure,
And have a heavy master to obey,
My last struggle rages, death lies in store,
How hard upon David shall this crown weigh?
Slay me, my life is over, let it end
By an Israelite, no more wrath God send.

✣ BATHSHEBA

I see her bathing, her hills and valleys
Are ripe for conquest, Bathsheba thrills me.
Her dull sweet husband with army rallies
Knows nothing, I flow into lust's arms with glee.
We disposed of him discretely, her man
Of less exciting times now safely lost,
The child was not his, however else can
Such scandals be dealt with, though at some cost?
The prophet is not happy, nor his Lord,
My baby sliding slowly out of life,
In my guts, a groove is roughly sawed,
Is this the fee for her being my wife?
An empty bed, where once he smelt so nice,
My son is dead, was this worth such a price?

𝒥 DAVID AND ABSALOM

Absalom! Absalom! My son! My son!
Why did it have to end this way, my boy?
Absalom! Absalom! My son! My son!
Why does this day your father's heart destroy?
I should have punished Amnon for his crime,
He raped your sister—what did I do?
I ignored her. Kept busy at the time,
Chasing other men's wives, neglecting you.
You avenged Tamar; you took on my role,
I was too selfish to be king, you thought,
Were you right? I am not my younger soul,
Which faded long before this battle fought.
On this cold dead earth, your life bled undone,
Absalom! Absalom! My son! My son!

♪ JUDGEMENT OF SOLOMON

My baby! Give me back my baby boy!
Even a harlot is allowed her child,
Her comfort for being a cruel man's toy,
For all the moments held down, defiled.
A long-lost innocence lay in my arms,
My flesh has known a loving touch at last,
Don't listen, O king, to this liar's charms,
My son is present, hers is merely past.
Let her have him! Oh, please just sheathe your sword!
Divide me from him, not him with it please!
Let him call her "Mother," just spare him Lord
! Leave him alive, I beg you on my knees.
My tender child to my breast returned.
The fragile hope of redemption yearned.

JONAH

All right you have made your point, let me go
Rescue the murderers of my people
Let me stop them reaping as they sow
Preaching at ziggurat's bloody steeple
I shall tell them loud your saving warning
Watch you pardon those monsters their sick crimes
I shall witness their salvation dawning
Those whose destruction I plead at all times
Assyria, God loves even you!
Who have shattered children against stone
Your skull-collecting souls he shall pursue
Even as you laugh when the dying moan.
Give me strength, my Lord, in this whale asleep
To dive through the depths of forgiveness deep.

♪ JEREMIAH

You made me tell the hardest thing of all,
The truth. Judah just will not want to hear
Anything but sweet lies, false prophets call
Being answered warmly though death draws near.
They want to kill me, faithfulness to you
Is treason in their sight, I am waiting
For your wave to crash over them, pursue
What I preach and am paid well in hating.
There is a future; you have told me that,
We must have faith; ah that's the tricky part,
As soon our Temple shall be pillaged flat,
While we wait for laws written on the heart.
I have done my job and now sets my sun
Though night shall be dark Lord, your will be done.

❧ THE WRITING ON THE WALL

What a party! Wine and women spread wide,
Gold Jewish vessels gave decoration,
My lords and ladies no pleasure denied,
And then this happens — a desolation?
Writing on the wall by no earthly hand,
I do not sense a blessing. Is this death
For me and Babylon? Do our gods stand
For us or anything? I hold my breath.
Daniel, you must know, the whole truth tell.
You don't look scared, can I take the blow?
You alone I trust, does this sign doom spell?
Tell what my astrologers just can't know.
So that is it, at least you did not lie,
I must thank you prophet, before I die.

❧ RUTH

She is my mother now, I cling to her,
No longer Moab's daughter, I choose
Naomi's people and her God prefer,
To a new land settle and old ties lose.
I go out to glean a kinsman's field,
His men do not chase away. His favour
Rules, he knows my story, I appealed
To his warm ways, and his kindness savour.
My mother teaches me, I come at night,
His feet uncover that he might be mine,
And cover me with love, my hopes hug tight,
He wakes, I tell my dream—he shall be mine.
A new son for Naomi, and new life
For both of us: I am a happy wife.

✿ THE WEIRDEST NIGHT EVER

This has to be the weirdest night ever,
Can we tell our wives? They'll think we were drunk,
Angels don't talk to shepherds, no, never,
Just kings and some prophets, they'll call it bunk.
There we were minding our sheep-flocks when
An angel told us of the Messiah,
Born to us this day in a manger, then
A load of angels set the sky on fire!
Proclaiming God's glory we shone with them
Then they left us swiftly and off we went
To seek our born saviour in Bethlehem
We found the dear boy and due homage spent
Let them call us drunk, he have seen true light
A new star shines here on the holy light.

🎵 AN INNKEEPER

I gave them the barn, they seemed nice enough
A man and his wife, a kid on the way
I let them bed down on the straw and stuff
And then I gave up on a long hard day.
Shepherds, they said. I heard other breakfast,
To see some baby, they came in the night,
All a bit odd, funny stories spread fast
Of angels in the sky, dancing delight.
Then there were foreign gentleman flocking
Giving gifts like gold to the guest's new boy
This looked serious, there could be no mocking
How would the future this rare child employ?
They paid their bills and left, it had been fun
Now I wonder what happened to their son?

❧ HEROD

What am I supposed to do, crown the Brat?
Strange men from the east strange, mad stories tell,
We must take action, crush such rumours flat,
To protect our power, that fragile shell.
Do what needs to be done at Bethlehem,
A star has risen—blot it out quickly,
Tear out the roots and crush the Infant stem,
Kill all infants, let their blood run thickly.
Don't look at me like that, all mortal thrones
Are painted bright with blood, all earthly might
Builds palaces chiefly of human bones,
Our swords shall win and men shall call it right.
Life can be difficult, maybe we're scum,
But how else can we save my own kingdom?

❧ JOHN THE BAPTIST

The wilderness is an unworldly place,
In the dust-pool visions dive into you
And swim around your mind. Storms scourge your face
And devour your soul all the way through.
Locusts and wild honey, a fit diet
For a prophet I suppose, still I miss
Bland normal bread, in the desert quiet
I strain to the call above sand-breeze hiss.
Who will he be? Who is this messiah
Who I must proclaim? Who shall believe him?
No voice informs me, a crow low flyer
Goes before me to the horizon-rim.
Jordan's banks are waiting, I must baptize
Whoever is sent to open earth's eyes.

☙ A POST-TEMPTATION ANALYSIS

The wretch just doesn't see I'm right for him,
Why won't he just magic stone into bread?
The ways of his Dad need a little trim,
My own path offers an easier tread.
Hop off the temple, give people a show
And those angels something to do I said
Would he listen? Well of course he said no
I'm telling you know that he'll end up dead.
All the kingdoms of the earth, all I could
Give him, were his if he'd be sensible
Was he hell! No due worship to me would
Leave his thin lips thick with pious dribble.
What can he do? Can he kill sin and death?
Can he rise from the dead? Don't hold your breath!

♪ REDEMPTION

Cheap perfume masking scent of cheaper men,
Towards my redemption, I approach,
Braving hypocrisy's white-washed den,
Its scorn and lust curdle as reproach,
I enter, eyes of flint cut judgement's mark,
But I kneel down and set upon my task,
Of adoration, though Pharisees bark,
And snicker, at the blessings from my flask.
He defends me, the first to take that strain
In my whole life, gives love's redeeming gaze,
Over lifelong landscape of shame and pain,
Wiping out tears of despairing days.
I go away, accepted by my Lord,
While others stay, and reap their own reward.

❧ SAMARITAN WOMAN

Heat-trodden hardness stinging into foot,
Labouring under sun's skin-parching glare,
Lumbering her water-jug along rut,
Carved by those who would despise and stare.
Another outcast standing by, a Jew,
Looks into her and begins to speak,
He dares to read her soul right through,
A fortress of sorrows begins to creak.
Hard tar-lumps of hostility dissolve,
More personal resentments now retire,
The strange man fills her with a new resolve,
Gives her the taste of eternal desire.
Running to make love's revelation heard,
She drinks the living waters of the Word.

❧ A RICH MAN'S LAMENT

I did nothing, why are you blaming me
For that scabby beggar once sat outside
What happened to be my gate? Why me?
Burning while he stands on the other side.
Lazarus, is that your name? please assist
My good man. Abraham, please remember
Enough compassion slightly to resist
The fire-cloud trying me to dismember
Oh dear, can't you warn my brothers in time?
If the law and the prophets are so strict
To make common callousness such a crime
Then Lazarus must not be derelict.
He can't warn? Then woe for them when they're dead
If this awaits those who do not share bread.

❧ DAUGHTER OF CANAAN

Waiting in the heavy heat, I look out,
For my thin thread of hope, the healing Jew,
Who should despise me, yet I do not doubt,
That He shall save my child — He comes to view.
I fall down, all dignity cast aside,
My open wound I bear for all to see,
He calls me a dog but I hug no pride,
Just beg some scraps to end my misery.
He sees my faith, such faith as saves,
His dog becomes His daughter, I believe,
And He believes in me, my joy He craves,
And Israel's flock shall this Lamb receive.
When all else failed, I dared to try,
God's mercies as you must — cling on and cry.

♪ NO STONE CAST

He fled from me, left me to take the blame,
They dragged me out for satisfaction,
To cast their sins at scapegoat of ill fame,
Readying themselves for brutal action.
They brought me to the weirdo stopping by,
Asked him what to do with me, he bent,
Writing in the dust. Did my sentence lie
With this mad prophet? Would my life be spent?
He got up, told the sinless one to cast,
The first stone against me, that shut them up,
The grey-beards went first, then the young ones fast,
Just us two left, I drank from mercy's cup.
None could condemn me, so he set me free,
To sin no more and God's own lover be.

✣ MARTHA AND MARY

She just sat there listening, that was all
He wanted, not heavy meals, or deep sighs
Of self-martyrdom, just to hear his call
Was all he asked for, with patient eyes.
Drinking from his well, the kind Gospel clear
She washed in his crystal pool of love
Letting him teach her to new music hear
Song of salvation sung through grace above.
Martha was angry, whining about her,
Why did he not order her to her chores?
Yet there was just one thing he would prefer
Of her, to stop and swim in his wise laws.
He does not want our frenzy, just our hearts
To rest in him. Lay down the lesser parts.

🌿 ZACCHAEUS

Squeezing blood from stone was my employment,
Collecting Rome's taxes from grudging hands,
Grinding men's faces for my enjoyment,
As their women cried at my demands.
Things were noisy that day, business was slow,
Crowds were clogging streets, I went up a tree
To get a better look, he would soon go
Past me, whoever he was I would see.
He came, looked at me, wanted to stay
At my home, my own brothers would not touch
My shadow, he wished to spend his day,
With me the leech. I could not bear this much.
After this gift, I could not count a cost,
The Son of Man had come to save the lost.

☙ DELIVERANCE

Splinters of broken thought piercing my skin,
Demons dancing in my head, calling names,
Sharp-toothed parasites wearing me thin,
Gashing into my flesh with stone that maims.
Their name was legion. Marching me away
From life, to tomb yard wanderings in chains,
Eroding my identity each day,
A foaming frenzy polluting my veins.
He came, the spirits shrieking out in dread,
Pleading him to cast them out into swine,
They drained from me, drowning the herd dead,
Meeting a destruction that was not mine.
I sat with my saviour, new life to find,
Dignity-clothed, in my own right mind.

☙ LEPER

Leper! A stalking curse upon all eyes,
That used to be a human being,
Now walks for all to stare at and despise,
A sponge for loathing and worried seeing.
Strangers deride me, old friends just ignore,
The thing disintegrating in their sight,
I am now cast out under ancient law,
Dead to them, except as a tool of fright.
A healer, I had heard stories of him,
I trust not phoney, this my one last chance,
I beg of him, squeezing my one hope slim,
I feel an earthquake in his words and glance.
Clean completion, soul and body pure,
My death is over, God's mercy is sure.

🌿 BLEEDING WOMAN

Shame trickling down from between my legs,
Walking impurity stirring disgust,
Doctors have just left me to my last dregs,
My money spent with almost all my trust.
A crowd clings to my salvation,
I reach out to touch him, to dam my flood,
For I am a daughter of his nation,
He shall release me from my endless blood.
I touch his cloak. Power pulsing healing,
He asks who has touched him, I tell
My story, revealing my pain kneeling,
How he has dragged me out from my hell.
My faith has made me well, I go in peace,
To stand accepted as my torments cease.

♪ NOW I SEE

They talked about me as I sat there,
Black jokes and regrets of my existence,
I felt how they would grimace, point and stare,
While I tried to beg my subsistence.
He put mud on my eyes to wash away,
In a pool nearby, to end my long night,
Sun shone through my window, into first day
Of a new creation, let there be light.
Pharisees shook their heads, it would not do
To give Sabbath rest to blindness, my woe
Was sad, but mercy must know rules. No true
Jew would act like this, they claimed to know.
This I knew, though they all were blind to me,
He who was once blind could now at last see.

꧁ BETHESDA

For thirty-eight years I was laid waiting,
Thirty-eight years in this misery lain,
Thirty-eight years of hope left abating,
So I sink alone in my sea of pain.
I have no friends or family to aid,
I crawl to the pool too slowly, failing
To reach healing, and so my life shall fade,
An old joke of Bethesda flailing.
Do I want to be made well? Asks some man,
Of course I do, if wanting made it so
I would be well; he acts as if he can
Make it, tells me to move and off I go.
Rolling up my mat I begin to walk
As others gather, too amazed to talk.

A PHARISEE NOTICES A TAX-COLLECTOR

I bought up my God at a deluxe sale,
He fits snugly in my pocket, clinking
With my loose change, a most amusing tale,
Here is no cross or bitter-wine drinking.
My God is easy, always telling me
That I am right (he's less sure about you),
Does not deny me opportunity,
To glorify myself (and despise you).
He shows my reflection so prettily,
Blessing my light words and rock-hard actions,
As I judge my neighbour oh so wittily,
Urging God's wrath against your infractions.
I glide from the Temple all safe and sound,
While you still slobber (for shame!) on the ground.

AN OLD MEMORY

I could not follow you, good teacher, why
Demand what I could not safely afford?
Amid my riches in mourning I lie,
Thinking of when you might have been my Lord.
I was young but prudent, you had something
Worth having, I want to ask your advice,
To have eternal life worth investing.
To follow your footsteps past death's device.
Why did I call you good? I had the law
And the prophets, to give up all I had,
That I might walk with you through heaven's door,
Was more than I could bear, I left you sad.
Now I am old, old paths I must pursue,
Wishing I'd been crazy and gone with you

❦ NICODEMUS

I came to him at night, questions gnawed
At the base of my skull. Who was this roar
Of thunder? Who was this so-called Lord?
Who silenced scholars and struck crowds with awe?
To see the Kingdom of God we must be born
A second time. What riddle was this then?
Were our mothers to once again be torn,
By us, once babies, now full-grown men?
Born through the Spirit from above he said,
He brought to earth unearthly things indeed,
Strange distant heaven swam into my head,
Was this redemption that hope's laws decreed?
I went from him to ponder my odd gains,
Bracing myself for new love's labour pains.

PRODIGAL

I could not wait for the old fool to die,
Demanded inheritance in advance,
Went off to brighter lights, my luck to try,
Hard liquor to drink, brash women to dance.
It was good while it lasted, then the end
Of the party came, I paid up my bill,
Feeding the pigs, starved without a friend,
Desperation burned in my stomach ill.
I would go back, plead a hired man's wage,
I slunk back home to beg a mouldy crust,
He ran up to me, I could see no rage
In his features, just love's unbroken trust.
Though my brother snarled, I felt no pain,
I was brought under forgiveness's reign.

❧ TRANSFIGURATION

We went up the mountain knowing
Something might happen: well indeed it did.
He started praying, his glory flowing,
Light like a thousand suns: a truth unhid.
Elijah and Moses stood with him,
I wanted to build dwellings for them,
As the dazzling whiteness made my head swim,
Was this my Lord? My mind snapped at the stem.
He was the Son, the beloved, we must
Listen to him the voice said — said my God
My Christ, son of the living God, my trust,
A living vision before death was trod.
He lives and glows again, we too shall glow,
In his light forever, his glory show.

❧ PALM SUNDAY

Riding on a donkey fit for a King,
Unlike all others, passing through the crowd,
Cheering you on, their cheap hosannas ring,
Which shall sour into condemnation loud.
You ride into Death's Kingdom, to the grave,
To raze the sorry mountains of our sin,
To spirits in prison a new path pave,
And against the Devil your triumph win.
You see the traitors in your midst and still,
You carry on, seeing your bitter death,
Determined to do your Father's will,
To bear all agony with dying breath.
Riding your donkey journeying true,
Give me the grace Lord to journey with you

✤ MAUNDY THURSDAY

Lamps burning low in the evening cold,
In an upper room they sit down to eat,
He washes clean their feet, love's service told,
Before their betrayal which he must greet.
Ashen ecstasy, dying so to live,
His body's fragments passed all around,
Even to the teeth of Judas they give
Their power, to judgement's decree resound.
From his cup they drink, from this promised vine,
Of which they are branches that soon shall break,
They shall stand in need of redemption's wine,
To wash them once more for love's name's sake.
It is time, into the garden of tears
To go, and consummate all brooding fears.

GETHSEMANE

The cup of pain brought to my lips this night
An ordained offering of bitter wine
Tomorrow's battle grips my stomach tight
Dread and obedience in prayer combine.
I must drink its dregs, swallow searing gall
Dozing disciples take their callous nap
While I stay up to be betrayed by all
Denials rushing up like burning sap.
Alone, no cheering crowds, hosannas loud
Just my Father's will, the heaviest crown
His graveyard garden and sky's sunless shroud
I wait for them to come and take me down.
Now is the power of darkness, now glances
Glint at my face — now Judas advances.

JUDAS

I did not want to do it, no pleasure,
In killing that madman's vain talk of peace,
I did not do it for passing pleasure,
I just wanted to make Rome's tyranny cease.
We need power. I came to him in hope,
That he could give old Israel new birth,
I wanted easy answers, could not cope,
With his promised Kingdom's unearthly worth.
He would not lead a Kingdom like this world,
Nor know that we must live by might alone,
I went to sell him, buy a better world,
For a slave's price – let foolish Peter groan.
But now a greater anguish burns unhealed,
And I yearn to die in this potter's field.

🌼 PETER

It was not meant to be like this, this fear,
Watching him from a distance go to die,
I was meant to save him, that much was clear,
Not cower at servant-girls and just lie.
We all fled. After all our bloated boasts,
That we would fight for him, we go do that,
The blazing memory my conscience roasts,
Hopes of heroism had fallen flat.
He warned me that I would run from him,
When the time came, that we would all scatter,
I was too proud, my eyes to see too dim,
To know that my daydreams would not matter.
A cock now crowing shrill, a piercing knife,
To save my skin I sold the Prince of Life.

♪ PILATE

What was that man? Not mad, I knew that sort,
No freedom fighter I could understand,
Like those other wretches before me brought,
Whose blood my Roman duties did demand.
He spoke of truth, what business that of mine?
They called him a King, what Kingdom this?
Not of this earth he said, what Kingdom fine,
Made him abandon all life's tender bliss?
I tried to save him, but they wailed,
For his destruction, I had to obey,
Washed my hands of him, but it failed,
A building burden borne by me each day.
Clinging to my old gods I dread to look,
Back at the gentle Jew whose life I took.

♫ A BANDIT'S TALE

And so it ended, my fine old career,
A bandit's life is rarely a long one,
Hung up on a gibbet for all to leer,
My pleasures of booty had truly gone.
My friend on the left, some fruitcake between,
The would-be King now wearing crown of thorn,
They mock him most, priests stirring up the scene,
Even my mate finds strength to spit out scorn.
At last I cough up pity; then I see,
Those eyes seeing everything, then I know,
Who this is, who gives out his strange decree,
Sending me where I did not mean to go.
And so, instead of those who should have known,
The robber Dismas stands near heaven's throne.

✿ CENTURION

Another native above his station,
Needing to be taught a simple lesson,
Lest others be led into temptation,
Convicted quickly in late-night session,
We put him in his place, duly mocked
We raise him from the earth onto hard wood
Him who our great order would have rocked
Nail him to die, choking on his own blood.
He breaths his last, jeering turns to silence
Sky inks to blackness, the air drops dead
The crowd struck dumb by noiseless violence
Whose life is this which we so roughly bled?
Then through my bones a lightning bolt has run
That I have just killed God's holy son.

❧ IT IS FINISHED

My sweet Jesus, no one can hurt you now
Resting peacefully in your mother's arms
She holds you lovingly, wondering how
They thought you could deserve all this? What harms
You inflicted by your curing of the sick
By preaching riches to the poor and hope
To the hopeless, to stop misery quick
And broaden people to divine scope?
It is over, our debt to death is paid
Death dies with you, its castles you pull down
To rubble, where our evils shall be laid
And sack of squandered yesterdays will drown
Rising in resurrection, you will reign
Over our new lives, and never die again.

☙ HE IS RISEN

The lamb born to be slain, alive once more,
Springing over barbed wire of grave,
The pale corpse frozen in agony raw,
Thawed by the spirit's quickening wave.
Into death's rotting shadows he dived,
To bowels indigesting the dead,
He broke their bondage and their joy revived,
Old Adam's tears were no more to be shed.
When I am tempted to renounce all trust,
In love's final victory, I recall,
That for my sake, into the tomb he thrust,
Himself, and by his death bought death's own fall.
The sun has risen, forever to shine,
Night-time has ended, let this day be mine.

❧ ON THE WAY TO EMMAUS

They had killed him. Our hopes had died
On that barren hill, our redeeming King,
Judged like a gangster and crucified,
Israel's dream they dead degraded fling.
A stranger joined us on our way back,
Asking why we looked about so bleakly,
Was this a joke? What made our hearts so black
We told, and empty tomb rumoured weakly.
He shocked us, from prophets preaching,
A Gospel foreign to our ears of pain,
That the Lord must suffer was his teaching,
That through the grave he would reach out and reign.
He took some bread with us, in blessing spoke,
We now saw clearly: our despair Christ broke.

❧ THOMAS

What is this madness? Women's gossip wild,
Swirling in the gutters of our heartache,
He is dead. Let him rest in peace, the child,
Picking up the pieces of his sweet mistake.
He would not learn the world's ways, would not fight
With its weapons, he could not save himself
Who wished to save the world, I know right
He could not save it. I saved myself.
Of course you saw him, grief distorts the eyes,
The waking nightmare built upon our guilt,
Gives false consolation, I feel those lies,
But not the wounded body's spear-hole's tilt.
And who might you be? Ah, now I believe,
My Lord and God! How could my heart deceive?

ASCENSION

He is gone, above the sun ascended,
His body risen to beyond our eyes,
Our years together on earth have ended,
We look with longing out on empty skies.
To baptise disciples of all nations,
Preaching his word to strange and hostile lands,
To rise against our old hesitations,
To be our saviour's pair of earthly hands.
We shall not be lonely, the Spirit nears,
Breathing love through us to be passed on,
The past confusion as debris clears,
Building up Christ's body now he has gone.
Though our hearts may tremble and tears deceive,
We must let go in order to receive.

❧ PENTECOST

Flame of the Father burning through the Son,
Love's inferno melting us into one,
Babel's confusion now at last undone,
Over sin's divisions the victory won.
Fall on us, fire of God, make our tongues speak
Your language, burn down the grammar of hate,
Make us a better dome of discourse seek,
To tell your goodness before it's too late.
We are a family, now in this place,
All nations melted into your wide sea
That is Your glory, now we see Your face
As it is, we kiss the Trinity.
Comforter from heaven, enfold us tight,
Shining out from us your saving light.

♪ TRINITY

The Father sings his Word into the void,
From the depth of his heart bursts out this spring,
Creation's waterfall by Spirit buoyed,
The breath of love enfiring everything.
He spoke his love through Mary, bearing seed
Sown for us, baking our redemption's bread,
By the fiery dove whose flame fulfils our need,
That at time's end no tears be left to shed.
Dead for the Father, through the Spirit slain
In spotless sacrifice, and through his breath
Our dead bones rise with him to dance again,
The three-fold cord ascending us from death.
Rainbow divine, one glory shone in three,
Taking us into your own family.

❧ MOTHER CLOTHED WITH THE SUN

Clothed with a thousand silk-spun sunbeams,
You shine down motherhood upon all earth,
Twelve twinkling stars adorn your head, and gleams
Of moonlight peak between your toes in birth.
Him bigger than heaven bursts from your womb,
Shepherd of all nations, sent from on high,
Son bearing salvation, no dragon's doom,
Can devour his strong sceptre from the sky.
He is safe now, seated at Father's throne,
Sin and death waiting at final defeat,
When from clouds he shall come to claim his own,
And fiery serpent incinerates sweet.
Glowing with tenderness, remember me,
Let me my dear mother, your best son see.

PART II
Petals of Vision

☙ NEW YEAR

I shed the old year,
Letting its skin skip off me.
A pale freshness shines
Possibilities glowing
A lit path to somewhere new.

❧ THE ROAD TO SPRING

Breath turns to vapour, bushes burn with frost,
Crystal puddles punctuating the trail,
On which the sun's battles are frankly lost,
As noon-day sees its thawing vigour fail.
Clear crisp cleansing cold, making safe the ground,
For dormant life hid in the seeming tomb,
What has been lost shall soon enough be found,
This icy graveyard is in fact a womb.
Winter's work is but to build up the spring,
To save up towards the impending flower,
To gestate the soon budding, teeming thing,
In expectation of its public hour.
What looks so fully fallen into sleep,
Is just new birth growing within the deep.

❧ NEW BORN

A screaming beetroot,
Wriggling as if in protest
At new surroundings,
Thrashing little limbs about
To the starting song of life.

❧ BY THE POND

By the weed well-ribboned pond
Where frogs croak their symphony
A reed like a magic wand
Conducts as the breeze blows free.
No heron bothers the fish
As the day gets out of bed,
And I am given my wish
Of hearing no other tread.
Away from office and town
Away from each swarming street
Away from old boss's frown
Is revealed a soothing beat.

🎵 A YEAR AGO

A year ago I swore to you
My love and loyalty
It tasted like the morning dew
Our loves naivety.
A day ago I reminisced,
Of things I'd said in vain
Then I remembered when we kissed
Once more I felt the pain.
Have my treason's scars subsided
All over your pale back?
Has your hurt with time collided?
Does it make hatred slack?
I stagger at my treachery.
I hope you have moved on
I shudder at stale lechery
And grieve that you are gone.

❧ A PARK REVISITED

I drop my bread at an abusive swan
And scuttle for shelter beneath the trees
Counting the summers that have been and gone
Leaving me thinning hair and aching knees.
Where are you now? Do you remember me?
Can you still remember our summer here
And hereabouts? Have years been kind to you?
They've not been very kind to me I fear,
No new horizons coming into view
For me at least, lost worlds I only see.
If I had known how time would be taken
I never would have your lips forsaken.

✿ REMEMBERING

A memory grits
Like lose gravel in my shoe,
It was on this day.
A life's half-orbit ago,
That she held me one last time.

❦ NIGHT VISION

An angel of the night came here
She came and took me by the hand
She wiped away each mortal fear
And gave me joy to understand.
She sat and sang new world to me
She sewed new stars into my eyes
She made me shine a galaxy
That lit with love vast heaven's skies.
That night flew through the universe
The fire of heaven sped me on
The dust of earth seemed ever worse
As soon my rapture would be gone.
She left me just before the dawn
Richer and in pain. Now so soon
Began the tears I cried to mourn
Beneath the cold steel apple moon.

✍ WORD-WINTER

The word-tree is bare,
Branches bent to emptiness.
A barren silence
Quivering in hollow cold
Can some tongue tell out the spring?

✿ THE YOUNG YEAR'S LUNGS

A blade-wind scraping
Shrill as a sleepless baby,
Into my flesh bites
The breath of the young year's lungs,
Marking the advent of spring.

COLD RUNNING LAUGHTER

I held your hot dream
Under cold running laughter
Forgive me darling,
Why could I not let you burn
And melt away my coldness?

❧ SUN-SONG

In the cathedral
Sings the first song of sunlight
Prayer is rising
With the sky's adoration
God's amber turning to day.

♫ NOW IT IS GONE

There still stands the birch tree, by which we made
An end to awkward love. We made our trade
Of stilted goodbyes then drifted elsewhere.

Elsewhere apart, learning to be apart
Who were once two halves of one heart, from start
Of hope's April shower which spring rains bear.

Our love was not warm enough for the frosts
Of life's winter season, could pay no costs
Greater than shines of summer smiling on.

Hardier plants can face the frown of cold
Hardier loves can face the frown and scold,
We had our season, now it has gone.

✿ ICARAUS

Yes, I was stupid
To fly too close to the sun.
But tell me really,
Would you not much rather fly
Too high than not at all?

♪ THERE'S THE DOOR

Was my love too boring for you?
Were my kisses too pedestrian?
(Or even too equestrian?)
Give me an answer, give some clue.
The seeds of youth I spilt so vain
For years on worthless shoddy soil,
The broken past brings blood to boil
In me who served your sorry reign.
Are you proud my dear of your prize?
Is he proud of you? Can he see
What you really are—how can he
By lust's eye your depths realize?
Your truth is falsehood I suppose
You swim in lies like fish in sea
Why did you have to lie with me?
Such questions taunting hindsights pose.
Now go in peace and sin no more
Or go at least them—there's the door.

❧ SEAGULL

Would you turn away a hungry seagull?
You may jeer, but this bird has got to eat,
Just spare a chip from your bag overfull,
I'm not asking for fish or indeed meat.
Do you really need all that food? I hate
To be rude, but you don't look like bare bones
Perhaps I could help you lose some of your weight?
Let's help each other (boy my stomach groans!).
So that's how it's going to be eh? Buddy
I'm no sissy puffin, there are few fish
Left in the sea, I'll have to fight bloody
For the sake of my chicks, I'll nab my wish.
I told you so, thanks for the chip my friend!
This seagull always wins to hunger-mend.

♪ DRAGON

It is not easy being a dragon,
Stupid men coming around to kill you,
Waving swords and threats spewn from booze-flagon,
Don't want to kill them but what can you do?
I would have liked a quiet life in peace,
I could have been a good slow-worm or newt,
Instead these losers try me to decease,
To grab their paws on some imagined loot.
I'm a big softie really, if they'd call
Politely, they could come in and have tea,
And I would show them round, no need to brawl,
Then they could leave me in tranquillity.
Yes you can see my cave; it's not too cold,
Just please don't expect to find any gold.

❧ UNICORN

Yes, I do exist thank you very much,
I just keep rather select company:
Virgins and pure visionaries, not such
As would thrust me in a documentary.
A real star needs to promote his mystique
So I steer clear of cheap publicity
It's not the gossip columns that I seek
Or interviewer's sly duplicity.
Legends sing my praises and Scotland brave
Bears me in heraldry, a symbol true.
Spare me your scientists, from them I crave
Obscurity, like my friend Yeti-Lou
You're all just jealous of my magic horn
So you go make out there's no unicorn.

A PARTY-POLITICAL BROADCAST

We are the parliament of owls,
Elect us as your government!
Drown out the M. P.'s brainless howls,
We'll be the people's instrument!
Our expense claims shall be skimpy
A mouse or two — is that too much?
On defence we shan't be wimpy,
Who'd escape our talon's clutch?
We do not want fine houses or
Expensive mistresses, we'll make
No heavy tax demands or bore
On the TV with soundbites fake.
Make us your parliament of owls,
You shan't regret it. Tell me who
Could serve you better? We're YOUR owls,
So let's begin then: Twit Twoo!

🐾 A TALKING HARE

Yes I am a talking hare,
Be so kind as not to stare.
If you'd like to have a chat
We can talk of this or that.

We can talk of wine and ships
Backgammon or Irish quips,
Weather but not politics,
Alchemy or sly card tricks.

Shall we discuss Stravinsky,
Over an ice-cold drinksky?
Speak human! Don't go all mute
To a hare of high repute.

I'm no circus freak you know,
As along life's way you go,
You'll find stranger things about
Than this hare hereabout.

Oh all right then, suit yourself
Faint. Such fragile mental health!
Lie in peace, I'll hop away
And find someone with more to say.

❧ PROUD CAT

Proud hunter of suburbia you roam
The garden jungles, each one your domain
And then you come back to my waiting home
For a feed and a fuss, a while you remain.
You seem to like my really, and my house
You appreciate good service I know.
You tip me grandly, once you left a mouse
And rub my legs just as I have to go.
I have had worse bosses, you are quite kind
In your own way, deep down I know you care
For your servant, you understand my mind
Sometimes you let me glimpse your own laid bare
Proud cat, who rests with love upon my lap
With love I rest with you, a happy nap.

🦋 BUTTERFLY COLLECTION

Butterflies on display, in genteel rows,
Pinned politely dead for our inspection,
This is your home now, for how long who knows?
Coffined in glass for your own protection.
Because a Victorian collector
Took an interest in you, swept a net
To preserve by killing. Some selector
Claimed you for a small museum's set.
Deathless dead bodies, providing their tale
For schoolchildren, tight in an airless case
Uncorrupted by life or decay stale,
A see-through graveyard that reflects my face.
I would not crave such immortality,
Let my flesh be dust and my soul stay free.

♪ A SEAL

A slick bobbing blackness above the sea
A seal's sleek smooth head proudly emerging,
And its two black round eyes beholding me,
Our two gazes into one converging.
Ah strange creature, how could I understand,
The world that is beating behind your eyes?
How could I hold your wisdom in my hand?
What wisdom have I that you might feel wise?
You go back diving into your retreat,
Where my eyes cannot follow, I go by
The empty shoreline with plodding feet,
And there are no more seals for me to spy.
But there still swims deep the shore's vision rare,
In my mind's eye still hunts that seal's sharp stare.

✿ IN YOUR ARMS

I shelter in the harbour of your arms,
From the stormy strikings of spiteful sea,
Your heartbeat next to mine, my spirit clams,
As on my face you breathe tranquillity.
Sailing for years for this, not knowing
That you were my destination, kind port
For me, heart's journey's end, love strong growing,
A coastal flower to blossom-fire brought.
The shore I sought over long empty miles
Of time and space, the water-desert wide,
The constant scouring for another's smiles
Is all over, my ship docked at your side.
I have left all ocean, and even sand
To rest in delight upon your dry land.

❧ ARTIST

All are artists: there is no exception,
Coals of creation glowing red within,
A spark divine erupts in conception,
As new beauty shines out beneath the skin.
To make love with colour, to carve out speech
In sculpture, build cathedrals out of songs,
To touch stars barely within angel's reach,
By imagination this might belongs.
The Spirit dances over our waters grey,
Defeats the dullness that grinds out our years,
Granting us freedom if we seize this day,
To paint our lives brightly beyond our fears.
Streams of living waters surge from the heart,
When we resound with universe's art.

❧ HEART-HELL'S CIRCLE

I gave you a kiss like Judas, then slunk
Into the shadows, slipping far from you,
From the cup of cowardice I fell drunk
Into moral stupor, my blood iced through.
There was no worth in my dishonest doubt,
Loathsome was my creed, a creed so creedless
Seeking comfort at all costs, whines about
Anything difficult, life sown seedless.
What payment for my treason? What treasure
Would be worth all this? So now in the sad
Cold aftermath I can take true measure
Of betraying you, my remorse rags clad.
You deserved better, now you receive it,
While in heart-hell's circle I inhabit.

♪ LET IT BREATHE

Love's not to be angrily demanded
Like a frantic loan-shark collecting debts
The human heart's not to be commanded
By emotional blackmail sobbing threats
It is a delicate flower, crushed
If you squeeze it too tightly in your fist
You must not have its consummation rushed
Or it can vanish like the morning mist.
Let love bud and blossom in its own time
Do not force it from its natural shape
Into unnatural death, or this crime
Shall make your victim seek the first escape.
Give room to breathe and give some time to grow
Or pain's all your efforts will have to show.

❧ WHERE ONCE CHILDREN LAUGHED

Skull of stone with hollow window-sockets,
Where once children laughed, though few remember,
No spare change left in time's empty pockets,
The roof rent open to chill November.
People lived here, quite ordinary lives
In most ways, had births, marriages and work,
Breathing and blundering with normal drives,
Before they fell under the reaper's smirk.
Built upon earth, to earth it shall return,
With the bones of its builders, as we wait
Our turn to leave warm bodies, this well learn:
There is no escape from the graveyard's gate.
Our life flies short through a busy hall,
Into something else. Can you hear its call?

🌱 PILGRIMAGE

So we begin then, you and I,
To climb upon our Mount Sinai,
Trusting in a revelation,
(It is not above our station).

Our coupling makes a chosen race,
Our law lit on each other's face,
Let no dark forces countermand,
Our hope Lord in love's Promised Land.

Though in deserts we may wander,
For a while and regrets ponder,
Still hand-in-hand we'll make our way,
As one being till our last day.

❧ THROUGH THE EYE OF THE NEEDLE

Through the eye of the needle dare I try,
To thread my life? Dare I? Pushing out strands
Of courage held awkwardly, doubts supply
Clammy presence, but wisdom countermands.
I must travel light through this narrow gap
Broadened by love, no baggage of grudges,
No more drab despair, side-step hatred's trap,
And ignore old envy's winks and nudges.
A soul must walk naked past tight slit walls,
Stripped of vanity, all left behind
That the great foolish earth great riches calls,
The desire of the flesh and blinded mind.
I shake out of old clothes outworn and start
To make my way driven by God's sharp dart.

✽ AFTER THE AFFAIR

Was she worth it? Was I worth it indeed?
Was anything worth this messy treason?
Those who once loved us our deceits now read,
What was our purpose, our guiding reason?
The name of love is often said in vain,
Our blasphemies torn from flesh-frenzy raw,
Murdering conscience with the zeal of Cain,
In cheap delight, paw met by greedy paw.
We were seen. The truth unhidden scorching,
Fat soft sleek deception, soon they all knew,
Our dark smallness met with fierce torching,
Sharp lights unveiling each desperate clue.
Nothing was worth it, ashes of hindsight
Fall down on me, no nearing future bright.

♪ STANDING ON A BRIDGE

Arching across dark jogging waters brown,
From dry land to dry land a bridge stands still,
Suspending me over forces that drown,
The surly streamings that could cause to kill.
I look over the edge, into the thick
Soupy river, its glugging song hearing,
A sluggish gloom as my memories kick
Against the present, past again jeering.
I have been here before, I have been swept
Almost into the abysmal torrent,
But my earth-held station I still kept,
And shall keep now always I shall warrant.
Enough reminiscing, the day grows old
With things to do beyond these waters cold.

❧ BRAUNTON

Braunton is my home, like family
It need not quite excite or entertain
All the time, its air enfolds clammily
Walking along the winding river Caen
Meandering along the village streets
That can't resemble Paris come what may
A bourgeois respectability greets
The dawning of another working day.
Bohemia has its charms I admit
On firmer ground my settlement competes
A charge of worthless dullness I'll acquit
This undramatic place has its right
To flower gently, my people are here
Productive if not wild, a decent sight
Green hills give blessing, countryside laps near
As tourist's cars pass through, a surging horde
Annoying and enriching, winter-wet
Summer a warmer wetness. I have toured
Some greater spectacles but don't regret
On the open Great Field I made my stand
Braunton is my home - I'm at her command.

A WOMAN

Grey-green beads of sorrowful mystery,
Attracting my devotion as I drink
Bad tea. The pages of your history
Unfurl a little, and I start to think.
Should I introduce myself? Take a chance?
Your sad eyes beckoning, might there be rocks
Under your rocks to shipwreck me? I dance
In indecisiveness, bewaring shocks.
Why are you in this café by yourself?
Have you been hurt by someone? Has some news
Been to etch anguish on your youthful health?
Beautiful woman, please give me some clues.
You leave, my question clouding in the air
Without answer, still trailing your despair.

♪ MISSING THE NIGHT TRAIN

It is too late; I miss the last train home,
The station shall be closing soon. Must I roam
The streets, avoiding drunks and their concerns?

Yes I must, the empty hours drag waiting
With sleepless voices in darkness mating
A disgust with desire that never learns.

It was a long day yearning to drop dead,
It is a long day weighing down like lead,
Desperate dreams now fallen with the sun.

Was it worth it? Maybe, we shall know
One day when all is past, now I may go,
Back to the station, a new sky begun.

❧ END OF SEASON

Another summer winding to its end,
Its half-achieved ambitions softly ease
Into a sort of sleep. What now my friend?
What should we do now cold winds start to tease?
The days curl shorter into colder nights,
That lengthen over balding trees, we feel
Our petals wilting, dawning duller sights
Ooze from the horizon to tread their heel.
Life is not one season, we must take
Birth blossom and decay as all one song,
Singing all the verses we can to make
Our contribution to what we belong.
The spring of autumn shall advance, be brave,
For we cannot defeat time's tidal wave.

❧ AN EPISODE

I sit on the rim of my sanity,
Gazing down into the stony basin,
As if expecting some new calamity,
A vineyard shrivelled into a raisin.

I want to be sick, throw up the blackness,
The coiled snake squeezing tight my gut,
I cry myself into hot-wet slackness,
While gates to a future clang slammed shut.

Emptiness suffocates, creeping quickly
Into corners like poison gas, I need
Fresh air, leave this room to feel less sickly,
I try another room, my longings feed.

There is work to do, I go and do it,
An angel's push sets me back in motion,
Leaving this mess for my life's benefit,
Swimming away from that sunk emotion.

♪ YOUR PULSE BEATS INTO MINE

Your pulse beats into mine its urgent call,
I kiss you firmly, now earth seems so small,
We are a universe stood on the lawn.

The air runs thick with heat and lavender,
Through our clothes conjoins our warmth run tender,
Your eyes break into mine their deathless dawn.

We shall remember this through colder days,
And darker years, the flowing laughter stays
Amid sadder music, the future pain.

If memory would die, it would still live
In Heaven. God to us please mercy give
To live your joy in us, our love your reign.

♪ LUMINOUS DARKNESS

This luminous darkness gently guiding,
Past dim deluding lights that deform sight,
In dancing stillness lies meaning, hiding,
From the vapid visions of passing light.

The silence tells a story beyond reach,
Of complete grasp of mortal hand or mind,
It overcomes our brittle cups of speech,
A song beyond all songs of earthly kind.

Reason is brushed with a quiet hush,
Before this mystery, cannot consume
Love all-consuming, in the burning bush,
Who engulfs further than our hearts presume.

In a mirror darkly we see the face
Which we can always love more, never fill
Our appetites to nausea by the grace,
That leads us to Heaven's holy will.

❧ WORDS UNSPOKEN

Words unspoken, deafening in my ear,
Should I have asked you? What point was there?
Your kind wary eyes made the message clear,
My love was a burden you should not bear.

Guarded sentences promising friendship
And nothing more. Brisk cheerful sounds pealed
From your lips that day, "Your mask must not slip"
You thought to me: keep anguish concealed.

I could not receive what you could not give,
I understand. My fruit held no delight
To your taste, I am most appreciative,
Though the moment burned in me like spite.

We are still friends; well, that is something good,
We write and see each other, sometimes now,
And I try to forget that long-lost wood,
Where I wished that you could love me — somehow.

♪ LUNDY ISLAND

Far-off fortress of stone and springy turf,
In remote nearness standing round the sea,
Against the thudding, jutting, waves of surf,
I look to you and you look into me.
You call me over wide fields of waters
Past mountain ranges seagulls fear to tread,
Your song seducing past mermaids' daughters,
Onto my shore, and your charm richly shed.
Siren of unfulfillable yearning,
I cannot live on you, cannot escape
Mainland reality, this tide turning
In me solves nothing, can't give me new shape.
The problem swims within me, I must part
From you, and seek salvation from my heart.

❧ A SWAYING COOLNESS

Strong-brewed sunlight, bleaching bare dry bones
Of creation, poking through drought remains,
Pouring heat onto ungrateful limbs, with moans
I climb the hill, a beetle with sweat stains.
Why walk now? What is my destination?
I look for shade, a truce with armed heat,
Whatever July's procrastination,
My unwise walk must find a mercy-seat.
A tree, maternal branches spreading wide,
I seek adoption and look for a breeze,
It greets me; I turn to take up its side,
And see a coastline giving salt-spray sneeze.
Below this mound there beats the heart of sea,
A swaying coolness singing loud to me.

♪ IN VAIN?

Hollowness shrieking out an orchestra,
In the loneliness of late afternoons,
I try to wish upon a dying star,
An idiot singer takes stage and croons.
Morning was an unripe plum, resisting
Taste and teeth, then the promise of midday
Came, giving nothing but hope persisting,
To hunger painfully for promised pay.
No moon tonight, no lighthouse in the sky
Shall guide our course, fallen in the dark,
We sleep expecting better soon - but why,
On rolling pebble Earth seek wisdom's mark?
Whatever reason for our creation,
Lies beyond my moment's contemplation.

✽ STUMBLING TOWARDS GOD

Pleading and resentment sweating out cold
As delirium. I mutter my sounds
Of desperate groping for love to hold,
In the darkness heaping burial mounds.
Rosary beads roll down my face and smear
My composure, I try to pray, telling
Some truth to God, the demons leer
At my attempts to find safer dwelling.
Pride is a painful thing to swallow hard,
Deep down the gullet of self-reliance,
My skin with smoking reality tarred,
Hisses at grace's sharp stern appliance.
God is truth, in him my falseness tumbles,
And I move in love despite my stumbles.

𝄞 UNDER THE WEATHER

Blank-staring sky, you ought to understand,
The grey muteness sinking beneath my skin,
Secreting drabness like some morbid gland,
A broken bag-lady sleeping off Gin.
Pinpricks of wind-sown water bleeding down,
From clouds not seriously injured yet,
A tree branch dancing tries to play the clown,
It is no use, the clouds to darkness set.
Pouring cold offerings with more coldness,
Waterfall drowning into shallow pools,
The heavens explode with lightning boldness,
Promising scarce safety for passing fools.
It is finished; the clouds begin to go,
I begin to shine, and walk a rainbow.

❦ BESIDE THE SEA

Rough-tongued wind licking my face with glee,
Like an over-excited Labrador,
I toss out some pebbles upon the sea,
Keeping my feet clear of the surging shore.
Sea, an oblivion in curling wave,
Drowning concerns brought out from leaden land,
This is the siren that wishes me her slave,
To her watery womb, few doubts withstand.
Back there is busyness, beyond the reach
Of the swaying sea-spray, we battle in
A thousand petty conflicts, yet this beach
Remains, tides timeless warfare not wearing thin.
Between the earth, the sky and this great sea,
There is this moment of sharp purity.

♪ THE WOOD'S RELEASE

Mortality mushrooms on oak tree's bark,
A teaspoon of sunlight touching roots dark,
Old roots remaining by custom still.

Birdsong ballads chatter through the woodland
Silence, a music earth can understand,
Written by blood by primordial will.

Life and death fermenting, here is its wine
Drank in the moss-breathed air. We can resign
Ourselves from self-importance, hold this peace.

My worries overshadowed by treetops
Covering me with care, my turmoil stops,
And I float in the flow of the wood's release.

❧ I MUST AWAIT THE DAWN

A morning afterwards, I wake and feel
An emptiness lying right beside me.
It is all over, thought try to unpeel
Recent events to digest easily.
It is not easy, losing you so fast,
You were my earth, your warm roundness holding
Me in orbit. This lifeless moon at last
Could taste life in your flowers unfolding.
Hope uprooted from your soil soon decays,
Am I to rot apart from you, my dream
Of woman? Thirsting for your gentle ways
Amid the numbness, I begin to scream.
And then I stop. In rage I shall not mourn,
My sun has set, I must await the dawn.

✽ EACH WARM KISS

The petals of your mouth unfold slightly,
And a thawing in my veins takes place,
I come now pressing upon you lightly,
My eagerness. I swim in your embrace.
The ivy of your arms grows around me,
Covering me in undying green, your roots
Penetrate me; you rest on me, no fee,
Just our delight as love breaks out new shoots.
I am your body and you are my soul,
Your breath sings in my lungs and yours through mine,
You are my compass, my North and South Pole,
As our fingers weave their tapestry fine.
We walk in Eden's garden, this kind bliss,
Running as a river through each warm kiss.

ROSE RAPTURE

In a vase resting,
An emblem of rose-rapture.
We met together
Counting the petals of love.
Here blooms red testimony.

A GRASP AT MERCY

Dislocated incantations rally
Round the inside of my skull, groping hope.
It does not oblige me, a dark alley
Beckons, is this a noose of hangman's rope?
Riverbed of extinct water, dead dust
Of pride and lust, my mind a desert plain,
Pert dreams shrivel and sag, the gods we trust
Ring hollow, those idols; earth's triumphs wane.
My sterile soul can bear no fruit, no seed
Can be well-sown by me, this bare dead tree
Fit for the bonfire, here no earthly creed
Can save, a higher grace must rain on me.
Out from the depths I scream out to the sky,
To the God beyond, a grasp at mercy try.

MOVING ON

A dead petunia trampled into mud,
Infernal cows are chewing on my cud,
Colours shattered into dereliction.

The fields of promise are now closed
To business, questions must now be posed,
By doctors studying my affliction.

The gate is locked, find another path,
The past is no true highway, nor sour wrath
For what cannot be undone, quit your bile.

A narrow way leading me from this grave
Draws near, which the stones of forgiveness pave,
I shove my feet, move on and try to smile.

🌿 FIRST DAY AT SCHOOL

Beside the oak tree stood a village school
I was sent to learn a little something
So I would at least be a literate fool
And on society not burdening
Unduly. In a cabin we took seats
The stone building was from another age
Too small for current numbers. She entreats,
Grandmotherly schoolmistress, the wall beige
(Once cream?) And then comes registration
Name, "Yes Miss," are we supposed to say yes?
Surnames ordered to our proper station
Affirming her call is what I ought to guess.
"No Miss" I say, perverse anarchic pup
Child warning what he'll be when he's grown up.

☽ VIGIL

Now is a time for timelessness, before
The dense ink-cloud of the night disperses,
Monks assembled by their monastic law,
Begin chanting their pendulum verses.
A mother rises in the dark to feed,
A sacrifice of love to her new child,
The monks in prayer answer our world's need,
Pleading redemption from our terrors wild.
Nightmares walk the earth, making us their prey,
Fantasies swell in shadows, we need light
To see love clearly, to see Christ's new day,
And daily battles win by his love's might.
To the Immortal King our brief trials sing,
Those monks who sing to God in offering.

❧ TO A BETTER ABODE

Lying on my tomb-slab, searching for points
To my existence, what bright future could
Raise me upright? Restore my broken joints
To health? This washed-up doll of driftwood?
Darkness is my mistress now, possessive,
Her fingernails dig into my flesh,
I am stricken (by some gene recessive?),
Viewing creation through an iron mesh.
I hear them building me a coffin cheap,
Lined with my regrets, I crawl away
With strength unknown, escaping restless sleep,
Through my black clouds there comes a kind God's ray.
I begin to walk, to walk my long road,
From this abyss to a better abode.

♪ I MISS YOU

I miss you breathing laughter on my face,
The subtle waltzing of your fingertips
Along my neck, how our kisses would trace,
Paths of discovery with eager lips.
Broken guitar strings of our ambitions,
To be as one, our vows made in haste broke
By the real world, life's stern conditions
Did not sympathise, held our dreams to choke.
The dew of your womanhood kept me fresh,
Now I am a dry tree, my sap is spent
Away, the communion of soul in flesh
Was worth it though, the heaven where we went.
For a time I was yours and you were mine,
And we felt a shiver of love divine.

⚘ LEAVING DURHAM

"You utter loser!" words assaulted me
From a car window in young lord's accent
With total failure he had faulted me
As into exile from Durham I went.
I was not called to be a monk or priest
Nor meant indeed to be a professor
Fir years I had struggled, survived at least
Had tried to be a humble confessor
In scholarship of what stood out as truth.
Ludicrous, pretentious, adolescent,
I was a gauche unpalatable youth
From childhood oddness a convalescent
My friends few and mad as me, needing more
Support than they could give, I was lonely
My shyness festering as bleeding sore
Not utterly lost, my one way only
To where there was refuge, my childhood home
Trying to salvage some adulthood, pay
Dues to society, for purpose roam.

✤ BEACH

Avoiding sea-soaked slime I walk the rocks,
Thoughts heave and crash in synchrony, I see,
A lonely seagull, which draws near and mocks,
This brooding scene, his distant friends agree.
Life carries one, just in a minor key,
The time for grand expansion has now left,
Drifting on the horizon of the sea,
Formed by departed moments, I bereft.
It begins to rain. I cannot here,
Continue in self-pity, I must go,
The future summons me, despite my fear,
That sorrow shall last, I who sorrow know.
All storms of life shall pass, we must move on,
Marking the most of it before we're gone.

♪ WAS IT FOR SOMETHING?

In the noose of night
Swinging hard, a dying day.
Was it for something?
Those efforts now expiring?
I ask as I go to bed.

❧ STREAM

A stream emerges, snaking impure glass,
To some distant predestined estuary,
From undistinguished fields and woods to pass,
Into the surging splendour of the sea.
An end from a beginning is not clear,
The mightiest things have simple birth,
The full-grown glories we now hold so dear,
Were prophesied once against bitter mirth.
We cannot see where certain paths will lead,
Streaming away, beyond our bounds of sight,
Yet the tree is foreshadowed in the seed,
And the stream flows on with determined might.
We know not always where we are going,
But nonetheless we must keep on flowing.

♪ SUMMER

Blue-green crystal sea, soft-stroked by beams,
Of white-gold radiance, nature comes awake,
Sun holding earth in his firm arms, she gleams,
Her womanhood ripens her fruit to take.
Strong rosy wine of heat, making blood bloom
A thousand colours, creation dances
In her bright dress, with the gifts of her womb,
To the beat of season, fresh breeze enhances.
Earth sky and sea, God's sequins shimmer warm,
On the glad dance floor of existence now,
The constant cycle sings its present form,
Before it shall be broken by time's plough.
The summer ecstasy burning down deep,
Must be enjoyed, before it goes to sleep.

♫ OCEAN

Blue-green eternity stretching from shore,
Rolling out towards soaring point with sky,
Splashing and crashing with a vibrant roar,
The sea keeps performing orchestral cry.
Why crash constantly against broken rocks?
Against the sandy grain? Why persevere
In this business? Summer and winter shocks
Stinging the unversed, though the wise revere.
The rhythm of the music dances on,
The rhymes and reasons of the earth, complete
A poem of the cosmos, wisdom shone,
From every glitter on tidal sheet.
Bless pulsing ocean, as our lifeblood's birth,
Icon of new heaven, and of new earth.

❧ ROCK POOL

I see a rock pool,
Kingdom of seaweed forests
Gaze deep into it.
Is my world but a rock pool,
Watched with care by greater eyes?

Kind sunlight kissing leaves into fullness,
Proclaiming Easter Gospel on the grass,
Erasing old winter's Lenten dullness,
Choirs of daffodils sing floral mass.
The tree of life blossoms into flower,
The frosts of death defeated by the spring,
Green shoots tremble with a new-found power,
Unburied hopes recover and take wing.
What slept beneath the soil rises to glory,
Dead bones of nature stirred back to life,
Preaching a parable of God's story,
Creation smiling like a new-wed wife.
The despair is broken, love's dreams made true,
Resurrection shines in the morning dew.

♪ DRIFTWOOD

Contorted water-sculpted monument,
On loan from sea currents' exhibition,
Bequeathed by tree's last will and testament,
And brought to shore to a new position.
Soft honeyed sunlight of late afternoon,
Shows this new art work to benign effect,
Before the dawning of the tidal moon,
Calls this old exile to once more defect.
How far has it travelled, this washed-up wood?
Along churning, groaning, toiling ocean,
How much more must it travel? How much should,
It labour under the sea's emotion?
As long as the sea wants this possession,
To adorn its shifting strange procession.

🌿 WHITE BONES OF WATER

White bones of water
Resting on a pool in peace,
Winter has risen
To claim his icy kingdom
And nature sleeps as if slain.

❧ LITTLE MERCIES

Sun captures a leaf
Setting it as if on fire
Redeeming a day
That before this had not shone
So spark out little mercies.

❧ LONE ROSE

A lone rose blooming
Loved only be God and bees
In hidden corners
Petals of grace spread blessing,
Unseen by the wider world.

✿ FLOATING

Leaves in procession
Floating softly on a stream.
I sigh a little,
Floating my spirit along
The slow flow of passing day.

❧ THIS MOMENT

I wake up next to you
And admire your sleeping form
Must we get up soon
To fight day's empty battles?
I kiss this moment.

❧ ADVENT

Another advent waiting for a star
To shine our way to Bethlehem, unwind
The tangled web of will, the gate unbar
To paradise now and a fresh vow bind.
Another year full of empty foolings,
Life wasted solemnly in dull pursuits
Of what shall follow us under grave's rulings,
Its posing importance hard death refutes.
Can Christ be born in this? Can Christ be born
In our hearts stable? Amid dung and straw?
Is there room for Christ in me? New life sworn
So long ago, is it still new, still law?
God's naked screaming love be born in me
Again sweet child, un-curse old Adam's tree.

✒ LET ME

Let me your sweet lips of cinnamon taste
Your marble beauty stroke with tender awe
Let us not now this sacred moment waste
Please open out to me your secret door.
Give me the blessing of your dancing hairs
Your dewy peaches let me kiss, embrace,
That I might lose in you life's brutal cares
Trapped in the amber of your bright face.
Moving to the music of your warm hips
Guiding me as I navigate our course
We sail in rapture, two entwined ships
As you hold me tight to ecstasy's source.
We shall complete, in each other's arms
Our aching love, which no sad shame alarms.

🌿 KYRIE ELEISON

If you should mark iniquities my King,
Who know me better than I know myself,
If you should mark each dark and sordid thing,
Then I have no hope of eternal health.
The death that does not die, the starless night,
The fruits of petty meanneses reaped,
The well of worthlessness, destruction's bite,
Await, in aching misery steeped.
Save me Lord, from what I truly deserve,
From all the empty idols of my heart,
From false masters I have striven to serve,
Allow new redemption to take part.
Into you embrace I escape from strife,
Your arms wide open on the cross of life.

✽ ENJOY THE SUNLIGHT

I want to go and wander
Near where the puffin plays,
My heart is growing fonder
Of sunshine and sea-sprays

I've had enough of mourning
For last year's fallen leaves
New summer is now dawning
And only the fool grieves.

Earthy sky and sea are thawing
So I shall thaw as well
Now chillness sleeps a-snoring
Till autumn breaks the spell.

I must enjoy the sunlight
While it is there to spend
How many joys of sunlight
Do we have till the end?

PART III

Another Odyssey

❧ ANOTHER ODYSSEY

Mad Odysseus makes us row
To certain death at double speed.
How much further have we to go,
Till into sea our lives last-bleed?

War is the toy of gods and kings,
For us to suffer and regret
We are but low-born wretched things,
Whom wives and children shall forget.

We left burnt Troy to return home,
We hoped at last to find our rest.
Combed out like lice by mother's comb,
Instead our sighs set in the west.

No poet shall sing in our praise,
We shall die like rats and no more,
Our King shall reap the epic phrase,
And we'll wash up dead on some shore.

❧ THE MINOTAUR'S LAST CHAT

I did not ask to be a Minotaur,
I did not ask to live this sort of life,
I did not ask to eat Greek virgins raw
Trapped in this maze—it's a mad sort of life!
Blame my mother; she slept with a bull,
Anything born from that would be messed up,
Being a monster is really quite dull,
Always the same meal without bowl or cup.
They're always running, no chance of a chat,
Always running away then getting lost,
At least the exercise makes me less fat,
I'm really quite fit as they find to their cost.
But tell me about yourself. You look sweet
And sour. Theseus you say? Watch your sword!
You could hurt someone. I'd much rather meet
You on safer terms. Ouch! Mind that sword!

CALYPSO

Men never know what's good for them,
Odysseus please stay!
Your kisses are my diadem,
Don't choose the bitter way.

Remain right here with pleasures near,
Beware the graveyard sea,
Immortal lips should hold you dear,
Be my eternity!

Penelope does not need you,
She has other suitors,
I'm a goddess, can't I please you?
Your taste needs better tutors.

A safe journey then I shall pray,
And wish, though I'm divine,
That I could crack to dust and clay,
If only you were mine.

☙ ARIADNE

I should have let that Minotaur eat him!
He was only fit for a monster's meal,
I thought he'd love me; he made my heart swim,
He could have saved me too, that was the deal.
Theseus, the name that ruined my life,
When I was the budding rose of Crete,
The day misfortune took me as his wife,
When he was brought as sacrificial meat.
I gave him string and I gave him a sword,
I betrayed my own father for that man,
Like a slave I served him as my Lord,
Then he dumped me here – was that the plan?
This is the price of my love unreturned,
Stuck on an island, my heart's strivings spurned.

♪ SIREN

It's not bad really; at least I can sit,
Which is better than the last job I had,
Singing to sailors has made me a hit,
"A voice to die for," that's not too bad.
Yes I admit there have been some shipwrecks,
But my fans know that's a small price to pay,
They sing from the rigging, dance on the decks,
And then jive down into jigging sea-spray.
They die happy, more than most on dry land,
Have they got anywhere better to go?
My music is heaven, please understand
That I'm worth all dark waters below.
I make a good living, it's not wrong,
Calm down and listen; I'll sing you a song.

❧ HELEN OF TROY

Plain features are a blessing, send no ships
Across the seas, drive no men out of mind.
But blood is spilt to honour my red lips
For my clear skin do men life's ties unbind.
I did not ask for this, did not ask
For mothers, daughters, sisters to taste grief,
I can't replace husbands lost, whose task
It seems is to please one, fast falls life's leaf.
My beauty passes but the grave remains
Though they'll dress this up in heroic song
No flesh body is worth such bloody stains,
Zeus and all may swagger, but they're still wrong.
In order to be some rich fool's chattel,
Must I see all good be slain in battle?

♫ HADES ON PERSEPHONE

Why did I do it? Well lust I suppose,
Made me kidnap her from earth's warm quarter
Dragging her down where black river flows
I took for a wife life's blessed daughter.
Persephone, would you not be my queen?
She would not willingly, her mother shed
Wintry tears and above no corn was seen
Her mourning hunger led man to death's bed.
A compromise was reached eventually.
Her bright skin melts my nights one third of year,
Even Hades wants warmth. Torrentially
I tried to make her love me. Came I near?
No, she cannot love me. Can I blame
Her for despising her grim jailer's name?

🌸 EURYDICE TO ORPHEUS

Now why couldn't you just leave me alone,
Safe in this cave of shady forgetting?
Could you not think I'd have views of my own
And wish to stay in this twilight setting?
Spring, summer and the harvest are all past
My bones are sleeping softly under snow,
Yet you still hunger for what could not last,
And back to earth with your folly I go.
You strum your lyre self-importantly,
Demanding all obey its order,
Dragging me from Hades. Won't you see?
I wish to stay within its firm border.
Then you look back at me and understand,
That dear death has become my true homeland.

MEDUSA

I turn folk to stone, what's a girl to do?
Cold snakes hold sway above my head and reel
Over my cursed scalp. There is none who
Can love me, none whose kindness I can feel.
Once I was beautiful, and that is why
Poseidon raped me. Yet Athena's rage
Ran on his victim before time to cry
For pity, thus my life began this stage.
Life? A girl is dead but a monster prowls
In her place with reptilian tresses,
All breathing joy turns dead before my scowls
Due to a god's assaulting caresses.
What can I do but haunt this clammy cave
And pray at least to find peace in my grave?

ATHENA AND ARACHNE

She was the better weaver. Arachne
Knew her own worth all too well. That vile smirk
She wore at me with those teeth and acne
But ugly mortals beat me at their work.
The muses can be cruel, though born of Zeus
I was not blessed as greatly as that cow,
Audacity like hers can make no truce
To genius so rude I could not bow.
Those tales she wove, of snared Aphrodite
With Ares, and her husband laughing on
Should peasant maids mock gods almighty?
Impudent witch your laugh was quickly gone.
Her work continues, I'd never hide her
Weave on my dear, you're my darling spider!

✿ MARSYAS

How could we let him lose? Apollo's spite
Decided the result, such a contest
Was never about music. The piping
Still keeps me awake at night, I'll divest
With caution what made men hard tears' wiping
Marsyas could not win, we heard a dirge
In his playing, the victor with poor grace
Fulfilled the funeral, performed his purge
For artistic ambition. All our race
Was taught a lesson: unsheathed of his skin
The musician carcass shone in the sun.
Apollo's sun at which we must not stare
The wretch played better, that was his great sin
(Such sent Arachne to a spider's lair)
And there are some who find this rather fun.

🌿 PROMETHEUS

The screams of burning children curse my ears
Was it for this I gave the gift of fire?
Stole it from heaven against gods' fears
Am I the one who lit this grisly pyre?
Each day an eagle comes to eat my liver
Which grows anew for torment, worse the pain
My ingenuity did deliver.
Monsters I created, can I explain
Extinguished forests, and plumes of smoke
From death-camp ovens, people worse than pigs
Whom I wanted to make gods? I must choke
On my arrogance, a talon digs
Tear out my vanity not my entrails!
I gave humans fire, set them light to burn
A brightest darkness, my ambition fails
Such is the legacy to which I turn.

❧ ATLAS

The weight of the world on my shoulders
Never gets easier to bear.
I hold this accursed of boulders,
And try not to look like I care.

I grasped to snatch great Zeus's power
To set myself upon his throne
So now with groans and sweat I cower
So now ring aches in every bone.

Pride pays its price; I'm paying in full,
The Titan who would crush the gods,
During my task I start to mull
The strokes of Heaven's beating rods.

My burden I must bear at all times,
No I can't shrug, no I can't flee,
She insists that I suffer for my crimes -
That hag responsibility.

❧ AS RICH AS CROESUS

"Count no man happy until he is dead."
These words honked in my head as absurd sound
No dainty flattery had Solon said
Its heavy truth would soon enough be found.
My cup was full, my treasury supplied
No, gorged, with gold, I was a happy man
I thought, my smiling crowned with King's pride.
Solon was right, Atys my son was slain
His glory fleeting fell into the grave
Then fell my kingdom, broken was my reign
From King of Lydia to Persia's slave.
All earthly leaves shall fade and take their flight
The only gift that lasts is heaven's light.

❧ MEGARA

My children are dead, all of them
Killed by my maddened husband. Why
Do I still breathe? The days condemn
My emptiness, wrath-drunk Hera,
Dread goddess, you cannot deny
Screams of infants hymn your era.

Hercules, why did you marry
A woman of sheer flesh and blood?
Hopes of long years a day miscarry
Because of divine spite, the whim
That against pity quite withstood
If only she had just killed him.

Gods and heroes, more than less than
Human, you make a fine story
Or two for idlers, sure you can.
At a safe distance darlings sleep
Hades is kinder, it's glory
Restful, to its bounds I'll quick-creep.

I will have my babies back when
Death exhumes me from this graveyard
He'll be all right, he'll make his den
In other females on his tour.
His kind escape with lives unscarred
Only bystanders bleeding raw.

☽ HERCULES

"Heroics" can be rather vile indeed,
The things I did to flaunt my lion-skin,
How many wretches did I cause to bleed?
It does not seem so fun now time wears thin.
Zeus is my father, that accursed state
Beyond my choice drew jealous Hera's rage
From birth she held me guilty for my fate
Before even, she's struck me at each stage.
Megara, can you ever forgive me?
I killed our children under Hera's trance,
This shirt of Nessus stings my memory,
Now can I die please? Death's a second chance.
If only I had been a shepherd's brat
Unseen from Mount Olympus. Snap an end,
Kill my mortal part, obliterate that,
Then to the gods I'll go and protests send.

℘ POTIPHAR'S WIFE

It's time to make a man of you my dear,
The door is shut; we're all alone right now
Let old Potiphar sink into his beer
You have a life to live—I'll show you how.
There's no need to be shy. I'll set you free
I have exposed myself, now don't be cruel
The longings of my heart must let this be,
Have slain all restraint in a bloody duel.
You will destroy me Joseph, please be kind
Such chastity is spite, let us be one
I'll be your slave with your soft lips you'll bind
With arms as chains, I'll be your trophy won.
Wretch! You'll die pure and barren, hard your pains
You'll learn what hate flows through Egyptian veins.

✤ PHARAOH REFLECTS

Such awful people, only good for sheep.
To call them slaves would be to insult slaves,
It cost us dear to them in comfort keep
At least their absence greater sorrow saves.
Foreigners breeding like rats, and they smelt
We tried to control the population
It was no use their brats rushed out full pelt
What could we do with that wretched nation?
They asked to leave; we should have let them go
Without a fuss, hindsight's a darling thing
Into the Red Sea's jaws they did us tow,
Before then dirges for first-born made sing.
That braggart Moses pulled some sorry tricks
Frogs lice and blood-Nile . . . *did* he kill my son?
Should I have let them go? Such politics
Are hard for Pharaoh, but what's done is done.
I pray we hear no more of Israelites
May Ra restrain that plague from other's sights.

♪ ABISHAG

King or not, his breath smelt like rotting fish
His few remaining teeth were such a state
Way back then I was quite a tasty dish
To be King David's bed-warmer my fate.
He was too old to do much else but snore
And dribble, in his sleep he'd cry out "Saul!"
Or mumble after Absalom, each pore
Of his beneath me sweated, sometimes he'd call
Servants long dead when he was half-awake.
Judah's grey lion let me stroke his mane
And told me boastful stories for my sake
But soon he could no longer take the strain.
He left me still a virgin at his death
No other was allowed to marry me
Now I can feel in my mouth his old breath
To his old age now life will carry me.
I must survey my wrinkled wasted form
Who's there in Israel who'll keep me warm?

❧ JEZEBEL

Why won't Israel learn from its neighbours?
Can it stand alone? Be reasonable,
Must my subjects resent their Queen's labours?
Prophets should not be so treasonable.
Almighty Baal, my sweet Asherah
That gruesome unwed god cannot compare
I shall not leave my gods though I am far
From their and my true home, this desert lair
Of madmen and bigots, Elijah's tricks
Coarse provincial, no sophistication
My Ahab should have crushed their politics
But he was too kind to rule this nation.
Jehoram may see sense, the current King
If he can keep a firm hand . . . he could not.
Jehu you say has struck him? Kohl please bring
I'll paint my eyes, how I almost forgot!
They've killed my prophets, yes I've killed theirs too,
Though not enough, their victory is laid bare
Yet there is one thing left for me to do
If I die it will be with dressed hair.

✣ ANTIOCHUS EPIPHANES

Everyone wants to be Greek, everyone.
Gymnasiums in every one-horse town,
On townsmen's tongues the language battle won
The knees of Asia bend to Greek renown.
Except for Judah, there some malcontents
Have proved reluctant to be civilised
We tried persuasion, and it made some dents
Many Jews saw reason we realised.
But it only takes a few. We sent troops
To enforce the law, to support the sane
Moderate ones against the tribal whoops
And Zealots' swords that wise words could not tame.
Reason! Sometimes it really is no use
They'd kill for their customs, their wretched law
Great Zeus and fine statues slung with abuse.
What demon made us ever these lands tour?
There seems to be no end, I shall concede
On my deathbed, indulge these lunatics
Allow their practices I have decreed
As my life burns down with the bed lamps' wicks.
By my crown, by my gold, by Hercules!
Why did I have to rile those Maccabees?

❧ GREAT PAN IS DEAD

Great Pan, is he dead?
Whose pipes play this new music?
From the East, tune blows
What is madness to the Greeks
With a cross its singing reed.

❧ BEHOLD THE HANDMAID
OF THE LORD

You could have said no when the angel came,
The Spirit would not rape you, would not force
Open your womb to strike our souls unlame
But you said yes to our redemption's course.
Joseph stood by you, did people wonder
As your belly swelled with strange promises?
Awkward innkeepers then shepherds fonder
Surrounding him on whom you clung kisses.
You knew there would be trouble, a sword would
Pierce you heart also Simeon said,
From Herod onward feathered threats of blood
Which you saw take wing on your son's cross-bed.
What you bore could not die, death laid to rest
Death's rule through him who laid upon your breast.

❧ NATIVITY

Turning blue, the baby's cries diminish
She is surplus to this civilisation
Exposed to Roman cold, makes her finish
Abandoned to remote desolation.
An Empire with no patience with the weak
Females, slaves, that marble brutality
Called glorious, how sharp that eagle's beak
It plunges to murder without pity.
Far away, as this girl breaths out her last
In Judea another child makes cry
This one shall live a while, an age is past
Another one is born. He too shall die
But in his death is birth of something new.
A child is dead, the might of Rome won't care
A boy is born, an obscure little Jew
The hope of outcasts and the strong's despair.

✺ EPIPHANY

Stars striking out in harmony
Against the stark waste-atlas space
From out a fire-fog nursery
Sings bright a beam to kiss earth's face.

Shine past our hatred and our spite,
Our busy nothings wasting time
Shine on our hearts a purer sight
That to the heavens we might climb.

Climb past the years along the way
That took to reach our puny eyes
Did one of these hold angels sway
And show wise men where mercy lies?

♪ TEMPLE SONG

Sweet terrible child, in you death I see,
Now I may die in peace, as death begins
Its departure from this world, fails to flee
Its reckoning by kindling cruel men's sins.
The world shall pierce your heart, you'll pierce it too
Your poor mother should save up tears to shed
She'll see you broken on a cross and rue
This day's prophecy when she sees you dead.
Because of you many shall rise and fall,
Many shall oppose you, many thirst
To drink your blood which you shall pour for all
Give life to some, to others judgement worst.
Take care my lad, God's promise in love kept
All nations give praise, though tears must be wept.

❧ ZEBEDEE AND SONS

It was a good day's catch on Galilee,
The nets heavy-full of wriggling fish,
James and John with me their proud Zebedee,
Treasures to market and treats for our dish.
Then he came, notorious now I hear
That carpenter's son who should do more work,
Breaking men from their families dear,
Is one labour that prophet will not shirk.
He called out to them and off they ran
Out of my life. "Fishers of men" he said
They would be, now their other lives began,
And on my boat I felt among the dead.
My hired men remain, but family
Became another man's that day at sea.

✤ CAIAPHAS

As a statesman I've made tough decisions
That one was tough, but I have no regrets
Thousands would have died had not collisions
Firmly been prevented, this youth forgets.
He had to die to save us all, that clown
From Galilee had only that one use
His death relieved the tension, that renown
The only one he deserved. Spare me abuse.
I stopped riots that would have sparked a war
Jerusalem was straw that could be burnt
So easily, I just upheld the law,
Were there other options? Oh no there weren't.
Before you put me to inquisition,
What would you have done in my position?

✿ ST PAUL'S FORMER ACQUAINTANCE

Poor Saul, I thought that he'd end up nuts,
His zeal was too intense, a forest fire
That could change its direction hard, so shuts
A once promising career, meets its pyre.
We were students together, well I knew
His passion for the law, hunger even
With loving hatred a stern Rabbi grew
Minding the coats as they stoned mad Stephen.
On the road to Damascus I am told
He fell off his horse and was then struck blind
Then fell into bad company, grew mould
Of that blasphemer's band which stole his mind.
He babbles false doctrine relentlessly,
Does anyone take him seriously?

❧ DAMARIS OF ATHENS

He was impressive in his unimpressiveness
The little Jew spoke of resurrection
In flesh. To Greek minds coarse transgressiveness
Could not pass philosopher's inspection.
An unknown God who has made everything,
We are his offspring; he shall judge us all
And dead bones into live flesh gathering
On judgement day shall stand said this man Paul
There were few takers in the marketplace
Just a few of us whom he told some more
Of one named Jesus, if his style lacked grace
Its substance was enough to strike heart's core.
No gilt Athena holds true wisdom's shrine
God not of human hands alone is mine.

𝄞 KING OF NEMI

Lying awake at night my senses lunge
Around in fear of murder in each place,
Until at last in sleep's despair I plunge
But then my torture continues in dreams.
I wake up just before I see the face
Of the one who laughs at my dying screams.
Priest-king of Nemi, guardian of the shrine
To Diana of the lake, such a king!
By killing the last one I made this mine
As my successor shall make it his own
By killing me as the traditions sing
His victory shall be my dying moan.
A runaway slave, I took my chances
Young and strong I seized opportunity
With my sword, now old-age backward-glances
At what was done, the bargain that I made
I did not take life with impunity
The price I paid to ply this sorry trade.
There is much robbery in an empire,
Mine was more open than many can swallow
But mine was the same blood-shedding desire
That in others is called noble, my joints
Ache today, the song-birds verse bells hollow
And I wait for whatever fate appoints.

🐾 A DAY AT THE COLOSSEUM

What are they dying for? What do they think
They can accomplish? I ask myself here,
Wishing for better circus acts and drink,
Who is this God whom they must hold so dear?
Why do they do it? Living is easy,
Better sacrifice to the gods than this,
Just say some words (that lion looks sneezy),
Just go through the motions — don't die like this.
I almost feel sorry for them, almost,
I could not believe anything that much,
To die like that for it, to make that boast,
Testing my faith by lion tooth's clutch.
Well that's over. How can this cult survive?
Can these zealots' deaths give birth and thrive?

ALEXAMENOS WORSHIPS HIS GOD

There we are safe from the respectable,
Stout slaveholders are seldom to be seen
Song's hunger cups as a receptacle
To catch the feast of God, feeding the lean.
A God for women and for broken men
The butts of philosophical disdain
We need no entrails or slain sons of hen
Or empty words that sophists wisdom feign.
Long are our hours of labour, short our rest
But on these nights we find strength infused
From our cess-pits we ride on Spirit's crest
We've tasted God whatever is accused
By gossips and the cruel. We shall not tell
Christ's mysteries to his enemies, we'll die
Death's sweeter than life and escape this hell
Forever rather than their deceits buy,
The demons they call gods, I have tasted
Immortality, forms of bread and wine
He comes among us, time is not wasted
In our gatherings, words cannot refine
What happens: but this I shall let you know
He hears our cries, us crucified below.

❦ EMPEROR CONSTANTINE

"Who is the most high God" I'd ask in bed
No moth or owl gave answer to my plea
Around in circles by that questions led
I waged war better than theology.
Nobody doubted my skill in killing
I'd make my mother proud, reign over Rome
All seemed golden but a chill thought filling
Who sits supreme above my sky's blue dome?
Great Jupiter or the unconquered sun?
One or more of that rabble from the East
For me such speculation was no fun
A man must act, to dither is no feast.
There were the ones that Diocletian struck
Whose Lord was stuck up on a gallows-tree
Is this the form that divine truth had took
The broken stamped-on face of infamy?
A sign I asked for, a sign I received
Upon our shields it stormed Milvian Bridge
"By this sign conquer" indeed we achieved
A whole age stood on its frontier's ridge.
What then? Christ's symbol had at last subdued
My enemies and heart. There was still ground
To gain in both respects, how I have rued
The blood that bathes a Caesar, there is found
Much in me beneath pagan attitude
Let alone my dearest Lord's, we do not climb
To heaven without help, Crispus forgive
Me dear son for killing you, such a crime
Torments this brute who has not long to live.

And all the others . . . God you see my stains
You see them all and yet you'll save me still.
You love me, what is greater balm for pains?
In heaven's fields as salve I'll gladly till.
Eusebius baptise me, wash me clean
Eternal life, can such a gift be mine?
I'll pass with faith behind this mortal screen
Take pity please on this swine Constantine.

𝕵 JULIAN THE APOSTATE

He stank of Christian enthusiasm.
Like malaria it would linger still,
His whole reign was one short breathless spasm
A churchy zealot whom his faith made ill.
Rebel children still bear their father's look,
He tried to organise a tangled web
Of myth and custom, make a creedal book
Out of quaint stories that should quietly ebb
Away with dignity. We had to laugh
At his preacher's voice, the lack of Greek taste
And Roman restraint in his classic path
Those sacrifices seemed a gushing waste
We nicknamed him "the butcher," much too much
Effort, lack of ease and grace, the sad state
Of the impossible, that man was such
As could but only be an apostate.

❦ ATHANASIUS

Christ is more important than common sense
I'll never betray the eternal Word
Son equal with the Father, no pretence
I'll make at compromise though I'm interred
Far from my home its sea and sunnyed docks
My flock with all its faults and saving graces
An absent bishop cast upon the rocks
Of exile, dependant on strangers faces.
My Lord without beginning made a start
The deathless one bore death that I might live
How can I gouge that truth out of my heart?
How can I grant another perspective?
God became us that we might be like him
So for my sake you need feel no pity
Immortal King, master of seraphim
In your courts is my abiding city.

ST ANTHONY OF EGYPT

You fled the wilderness of busy streets
To taste the hidden streams in distant sands,
The bread of solitude as honeyed treats
To hold the riches of gold-empty hands.
Demons mocked you beneath the scourging sun,
Battles borne daily, inward war through years
Of silted days, days God's will be done
Far from loud town-land's distraction spears.
You followed the lamb wherever he went
He led to desert's door that you might pass
As his defender, half the world was sent
To hear you preach that world's cares were but grass.
Christ is true God, you taught as his true man
And in your life lay lines of God's true plan.

꧁ SAINT GEORGE AND THE DRAGON

What can we sacrifice to feed the snake?
The sheep are gone; the men are thinning few,
We'll give him our children, draw lots and take
Who is chosen, the King's daughter would do.
It's her. No your majesty she must go,
For we have paid enough—what do you want?
Shall we send you instead? Yes you may go
Slay if can lead to blood baptism's font.
We could not kill him, stop the dragon's tooth
Is his God with him? Does that steel his blade?
It's steel enough, we'll take such Gospel truth.
The dragon is dead now our vows must be paid.
Blood of the dragon destroyed by Christ's knight
Brings water of baptism pouring Christ's light.

ST AUGUSTINE'S CONCUBINE

You loved me once Augustine, and our son,
The sapling that grew out of dirty love
Your mother could not stand me, she'd outrun
Our life together, you two hand-in-glove.
Peace always did elude you, you would read
And say the strangest things, not settle down
With me or someone else, you had some need
Apparently, I think back in home-town.
Whatever you do, don't regret our child
His first steps were not sin, I gave us life
Not death, a life you smiled when it first smiled
Always our son, though I can't be your wife.
Farewell my dear, I'll have no other man,
Perhaps I was also part of God's plan.

❧ ALARIC SEIZES ROME

All we wanted was to have our own home.
We've earnt that well with all the blood we've paid
To serve ungrateful condescending Rome
Against this city such a siege I've laid
That shall not be forgotten. Scribes shall scratch
Down this day in their Latin symbols.
Today we enter, no mortal can snatch
Mothers shall tell as they wield their thimbles
How the Visigoths won the world city
If they'd allowed us some far province
To rest our wanderings, shown us pity
We have fought their battles for far long since,
Paid with contempt. Their distant emperor
Dotes on his chickens, will not be a man
Upon my warriors his scorn would pour
Whose boots he's not fit to lick, no one can
Stop us now, we'll allow church refuges
A few days looting only, how they'll sigh
Who thought us their barbarian stooges
By German swords the pride of Rome must die.

❧ ATTILA AND THE POPE

Fear can be useful as well as respect
I find the two are often intertwined,
The foes of Huns know what they can expect,
Our very name's enough to break the mind.
Rome was waiting, there was the greatest prize,
We'd milked the empire well but there was more
Gold, slaves, spilt blood, a triumph of such size
That years would shudder at—a kind of awe.
A Shaman or suchlike came to speak of terms
This ended our advance. That old man's tone
Gonged firm, even a bold warrior squirms
At some things, my men had started to moan
Of disease and gnawing hunger, they went
Home without much fuss, knew they'd pushed their luck
Was this the limit to the Huns extent?
That frightful Leo . . . has a death knell struck?

♪ ROMULUS AUGUSTULUS

Would it have been better if he'd killed me?
At sixteen years I was beneath contempt,
A puppet-emperor from strings cut free
Packed off to exile, from death-blade exempt.
Romulus would not have gone so meekly
The founder of great Rome was not a mouse,
Should I have fought myself? Even weakly
Strike out against my fate so that my house
In history could stand with some small pride.
Even a boy should try to be a man
"Little Augustus" I was called, they lied
No Augustus would take this; the life span
Of empire must end maybe, if it must
Let it die a noble death sword in hand
To live in epic song, sacred our dust
And bone-shards. A German king gives command
With ease where strode the Caesars! What am I?
A small landowner starting to get fat
Was it for this I gave no battle-cry?
Rome's last Emperor is a bloated rat.

𝕵 A SLAVE SETS FREE

Ankle-deep in mud and sheep excrement,
Raising to God my hoarse desperation
In Irish captivity I drank torment
Druid's slave brought to despair's temptation.
I escaped. Back to Britain I returned,
Back from the dead I felt, home was my sight
But the land of darkness which I had spurned
Called out to me to shine Christ's true light.
A shepherd I had been, again this state
A force drove me, to lead another flock
My land of slavery through Heaven's gate
Unbind Satanic chains, though some would mock
I studied the Gospel and went to preach
In Irish tongue to Irish folk set free
This bog-soaked wilderness not out of reach
Of God's redeeming love, strong Trinity
Bound crowds, like twigs under Easter fires
Burnt out the lies of long error's ages
Full of a fervour which never tires
I laughed to see my old master's rages.
A cross is raised over the Celtic sun.
A Celtic cross proclaimed, the best of old
Into a brighter tapestry is spun,
And I am glad that a slave I was sold.

☙ ST AUGUSTINE OF CANTERBURY

A far-off island full of fog and rain,
Where the English live whom I must convert
Must give them the Gospel, its truths explain
And from their woodland idols must divert.
To follow Christ I must leave all behind
The life and people I know so well
To proclaim Christ with all heart soul and mind
To make his Kingdom in these kingdoms dwell.
Savages have souls too, believes our Pope
And we must save them, crossing distant shores
To bitter blood-stained tribes who need our hope
Whose broken-bone bought land needs divine laws
God loves them, and so for his sake must I
As I prepare to sound his battle-cry.

☙ CONVERSION

I have wasted my life on wood and stone
Years spent praying to my shadow nightly
Years spent gnawing on bare hollow bone
I cannot take this deception lightly.
Give me a stallion, give me a spear
Give me a chance to avenge my nation
Against dead dumb idols we need not fear
Let us destroy for a new creation.
Now light expels old darkness, we must burn
Our shrines to nothing, burn them to ashes
That is all we worshipped there, let us learn
Another way and heal our soul-gashes
No longer the priest of thin-air any more
I shall answer Christ's knock upon my door.

♪ BENEDICT

I am no Saint Anthony all alone
Though once I played the hermit in my cave
I am no wild ascetic, skin and bone
God trial of common living to me gave.
My life is with my neighbour, that my rule
God called me from the smooth humanities
Taught in Rome and dissipation's school
To pray in peace among calamities
Barbarians have conquered but the Lord
Outlasts all Emperors, Christ's gentle yoke
I bear as Abbot, lead with one accord
Both Goth and Roman, wise and simple folk
Learn here the Gospel alphabet so hard
It seems at times to learn and also teach
A monastery has no escape well-barred
We are from world but sin and Satan reach
Us, we can't escape ourselves, how we must fight
Fight with sacred armour, the shield of faith
Keep us at work and prayer; no pretty sight
Is the idle monk, here is no languid wraith
All eat and labour in well-balanced way
Our miracle is we live together
Each brother bears others infirmities
Wars and Kingdoms pass like bad weather
Still our psalms sing clear eternities.

🌸 THEODORA

I have done things to survive. Distasteful
Things, God may forgive what other cannot
Understand. Parading parts disgraceful
In public, stoking men's lust. Stir the pot
Snide gossips, it is me in robes of silk
Not you, you did not suffer and prevail
Courtiers dismissed me with their eyes, their ilk
Both high and low recount each lurid tale.
Justinian loves me, I love him too
As much as I love power, maybe more
It's pleasant after all that I've been through
To finally be loved, I waited for
Wide wastes of time to pass, favours given
Prices that were paid. Well we met somehow
Eventually into new start driven
As if sudden madness, look at me now
Dear former colleagues how can I express
The unthinkable? What you could not think
I live, Of New Rome I am now Empress.
There can be no going back, no retreat
From my rule till last breath, no idle mob
No scheming nobleman shall me defeat
I shall burst open veins make widows sob,
I am prepared to die, prepared to kill
The Lord incarnate chose me as his tool
That faith in his true nature I'd instil
And ease the burden of my husband's rule.
Hear how she talks! Yes I know how I sound
Sin has infested me dear, I'm not numb
But in such flawed ones is some purpose found
Hail Theodora of Byzantium!

❧ SAINT BRENDAN'S VOYAGE

The Son of Man had no place to lie down
Wandering like us, from town to town
For him instead we wonder open seas.

Waves pave their way through wilderness, the rain
No worse than Ireland's but gales complain
It seems at our presence, no home's soft breeze.

What is our purpose? That which made us leave
Blood ties and worldly warmth, which made us weave
A family as monks and new worlds find.

Whales ride, gulls glide, strangers and exiles us
On earth and sea might seem quite ludicrous
To creature's sight but God peels off glance-rind.

Monsters and worse than monsters — yes ourselves
Complicate the voyage, each monk heart-delves
Dives to the deep of man's corrupted will.

The islands of the saints the promise sure
Seven years we've spent, some died, we implore
God's blessing on earth, see high-heaven spill

 Where there is no night, Eden of the west,
A legend some say, not those who know best
Gemstone-pebbles, life-trees pregnant with fruit.

Drunk sailor's talk you say, but we've been told
By oracles divine so scorn withhold
Icon of paradise is our pursuit.

☽ ISLAM

From the desert comes
An army—of a prophet?
A new submission
Over the lands. A crescent
Shall we call this a blessing?

What have I done? Whatever is "crusade?"
Does this serve me right for trusting the Pope?
Mercenaries I pleaded, not parade
Of rabble who with chaos would elope.
Bigots and landless sons of noblemen
Who'd kill us all as soon as any Turk
Godfrey, Raymond, Barons infest and then
Sly Bohemond the worst, low Normans lurk,
None lower than him their Lord, God believe
I meant only to rescue my Empire
Give Anatolia blessed reprieve
No assault on the Holy Land inspire.
Byzantium has balanced centuries
Slav, Persian, Arab, Turk have failed to break
The ramparts of New Rome, now take their ease
To wildest dreams the Franks: a sad mistake?
Can they conquer all? From flea-bitten west
Dream-drunk with piety wrath and their greeds
Rome has sent this answer to my request
Well is this what anyone really needs?

♫ JERUSALEM 1099 AD

Jerusalem's no morning's walk away
Many the lands we marched, many the inns
For knightly glory and eternal pay
(The Pope had promised forgiveness of sins).
Beyond the west lay those tricksy Greeks,
With their alien church, no sort we could trust
Beyond them battles; dust, dysentery reeks
Still in the memory, blood soaked the crust,
Squabbles the heart of everything. We fought
Each other better than Islam but we
Hacked a clearing through bodies, what we sought
We found, I suppose, a journey's end for me.
In the Church of the Sepulchre we made
Our thanks to God dripping with blood spent
To no use, the defenceless met our blade
And was Christ's pain nearby so different?

✤ SAINT FRANCIS

It takes a wise man to become Christ's fool,
It takes a great man to become a child
To live not just to hear the Gospel rule,
The raging fury to become so mild.
You shed your gaudy clothes and father proud,
You left behind earth's glory and repute
Feasting on hunger, destitution-bowed,
You trod the painful path in Christ's pursuit.
Pain was your joy, poverty your bride
Your congregation men, birds wolves and trees
Within your body preached Christ crucified
And stigmata greater than eye sees.
Brother Francis, let me be your brother,
Kept close to Christ and his Blessed Mother.

❧ THE SULTAN AND ST FRANCIS

Allah protects the insane. That dear man
Raved out his Christian folly with much charm.
Leave him in peace, not since my reign began
Have I had so much fun, do him no harm.
They should send more madmen instead of knights
Those oafs who miscount one God into three
This gentle fool I'll give his babbling rights
Babble on like a laughing stream! I see
No death in you. This Francis is no threat
To anyone, let him go out and preach
Even if just to birds. We shall not regret
Be patient with the mad, may kindness teach.
Sultans must keep their sanity I fear
But what adventures with him I'd have had!
Risking all to say what we thought so clear
Why couldn't Allah have let me be mad?

♪ CONSTANTINE THE LAST

The city is fallen, why should I live?
An Emperor should not outlive his realm.
Oaths of aid by Latins proved deceptive,
This ship is sinking, I'll not leave the helm.
Jerusalem and Athens here embraced
Europe and Asia met centuries' hates
Clashed against us and failed. Now is displaced
That story by the weight of Turkish fates.
What took them so long? Like maggots they've gnawed
At our flanks for generations, this night
Like all nights was predictable: we're gored
There is no point in taking fearful flight.
I am Constantine the last, let me ride,
Into battles embers make my graveside.

❧ HAGIA SOPHIA

Hagia Sophia has lost her cross
A cathedral turned mosque turned museum
Though there are still many who mourn its loss
Do not think this place a mausoleum.
It was not Justinian's vanity
Alone which built it, spirit soared a dome
To reach the absolute, humanity
Cannot deny this longing, brave New Rome
Did not try, for all its sins it stood
And rose like incense, prayers can never die.
To gods known or unknown we feel in blood
Beyond ourselves a grace time can't defy
More than a tourist's interest we cherish
Sense of Holy Wisdom which won't perish.

ABOUT THE AUTHOR

CHRISTOPHER VILLIERS is an English Catholic poet, proofreader, editor and freelance writer who has written about religious matters for a wide variety of publications, both academic and popular. He has BA and MA degrees in theology from Durham University, United Kingdom, with a specialisation in the history of Christian doctrine. He won the Sonnets for Shakespeare poetry prize in 2015.

Printed in the USA
CPSIA information can be obtained
at www.ICGtesting.com
CBHW020314120824
12968CB00043B/497